EARTHQUAKES

by Kathryn Harper
illustrated by Venitia Dean

Contents

CAMBRIDGE
UNIVERSITY PRESS

UCL
Institute of Education

T0384556

When the Earth shakes

Imagine the ground beneath your feet shaking. Buildings and trees start to sway. Then the road opens up and buildings tumble to the ground.

This is what an earthquake is really like.

Rescue workers are searching for survivors in 2011 in Christchurch, New Zealand.

Big earthquakes don't happen very often, but when they do,
they can destroy buildings, bridges and roads.
An earthquake in Nepal in 2015 killed thousands of people.

Smaller earthquakes or **tremors** happen more often but don't cause much **damage**.

> *Big and small movements can be called earthquakes.*

earthquake

tremor

Why do earthquakes happen?

Imagine that the earth is like a big, round boiled egg. The outside is firm, but the inside is softer and very hot.

The outside **layer** is called the **crust**.

It's got a hard crust on the outside and hot liquid under the ground.

crust

mantle

hot inner core

outer core

The crust is broken into lots of pieces.

The pieces of crust are very, very big. They are called **plates**.

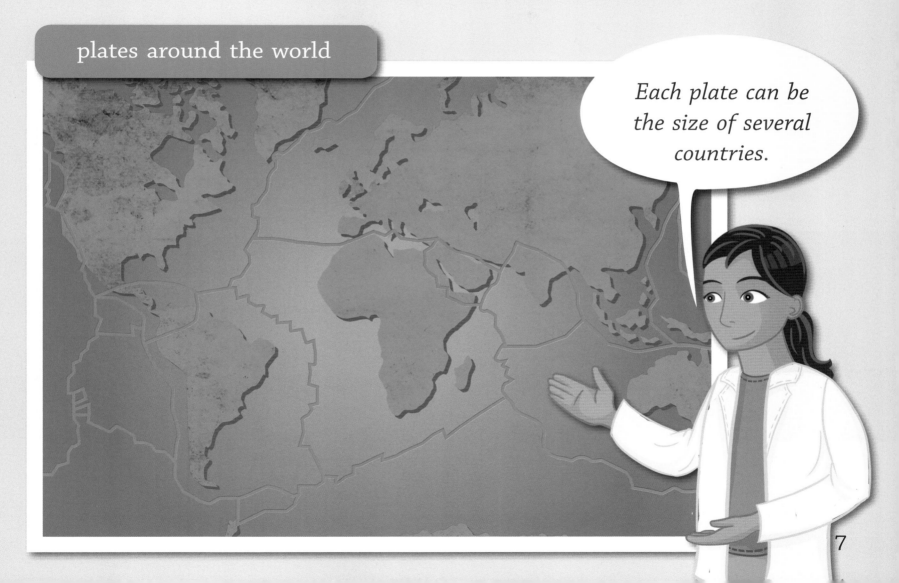

plates around the world

Each plate can be the size of several countries.

The plates bump into each other, making big cracks.

As the plates crack, the ground shakes.

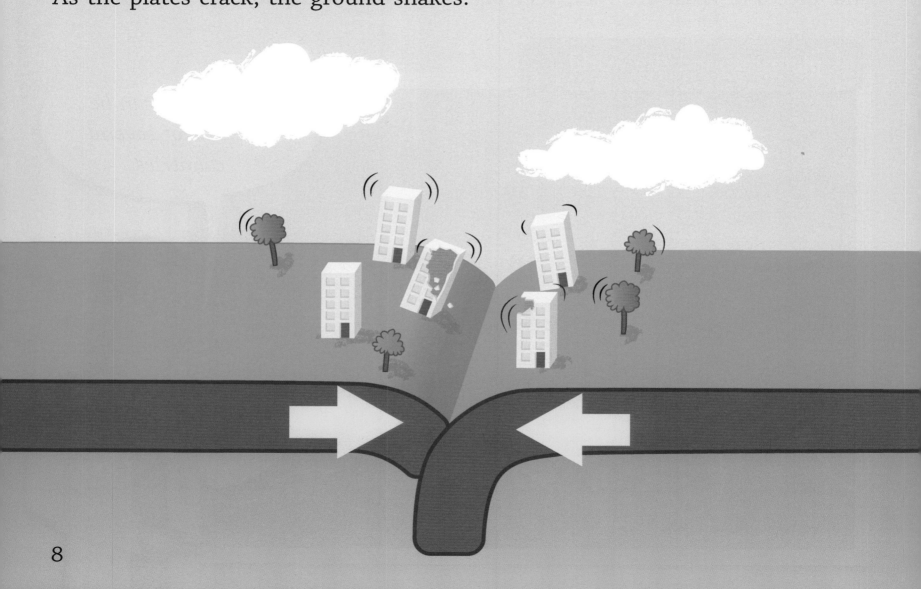

Sometimes the cracks are deep inside the earth.
Sometimes they are on the top.

Sometimes the cracks can be seen.

When the plates move, waves of **energy** travel through the earth.
These waves move very fast.

One earthquake in Tibet created waves in lakes in Norway.

The waves travelled a long way.

What is it like to be in an earthquake?

Earthquakes can be very small.

Glasses rattle in the cupboard and the ground shakes a little.

It feels like a lorry passing by.

Things may fall off the shelf in shops.

Sometimes earthquakes are bigger. Buildings fall down and there is a lot of damage.

Bridges and roads are smashed, power lines are brought down, water pipes are broken.

Japan

town on the north eastern coast of Japan after a massive earthquake and tsunami

13

When will an earthquake happen?

There are signs that an earthquake is about to happen.

Animals often act strangely before a big earthquake.

The ground begins to shake a little. This can last a few seconds.

Then the shaking becomes stronger and stronger. Things fall down and cracks appear in roads. Buildings wobble and fall down.

Sometimes mud comes out of the ground. **Landslides** can occur and fires can start if power cables and gas lines are broken.

15

Where do earthquakes happen?

Many earthquakes happen where the big plates meet.

We call these fault lines.

The most well-known fault line is the San Andreas Fault in California. It has caused many earthquakes in the city of San Francisco.

the San Andreas Fault in California

This map shows the world's major fault lines. It is called the ring of fire.

Japan

USA

In some places it was 30 metres high.

Tsunamis like this destroyed whole towns in 2004.

Earthquakes often happen under the **ocean**.
This creates huge waves or tsunamis.

In 2004, an earthquake near Sumatra started a tsunami
that reached 14 countries.

17

Being prepared

It's impossible to be totally safe in earthquakes but there are some ways to prepare for them.

Many buildings are made to be strong enough to stay standing in an earthquake.

In many countries, people are taught earthquake **drills**.

> *The best place to stay in an earthquake is an open field, where nothing can fall on you.*

Children in Japan and New Zealand are taught to get under a table or a door frame if they are inside when an earthquake starts.

19

Earthquakes cannot be stopped, but fortunately they remain **rare** events, and we are learning ways to protect ourselves against them.

Workers install special equipment to protect a house from earthquakes.

Scientists are watching for earthquakes all the time.

They can warn people when an earthquake is about to happen, so they can go to a safer place.

Scientists can use computers to find out when an earthquake is coming.

These lines show the movement of the plates so scientists can see when an earthquake is about to happen.

Glossary

crust   hard outer layer of the earth

damage   harm or break

drills   machines that make holes

energy   power

landslides   moving of soil and rock down a hill

layer   level of material that is different from
                 the level above and below

ocean   salty water on the earth that separates
                 parts of the land

plates   parts of the earth's crust

rare   unusual

tremors   small movements that make the ground
                 shake a little

Index

EARTHQUAKES · KATHRYN HARPER

Teaching notes written by Sue Bodman and Glen Franklin

Using this book

Developing reading comprehension

This non-fiction report explores the phenomenon of earthquakes around the world. The technique of a narrator serves to add information and to guide the reader. Non-fiction features, such as diagrams and simple maps are included. Some children may never have experienced an earthquake. For others, the experience may be recent and all too real. This subject may need careful mediation in such instances.

Grammar and sentence structure

- Consider how particular words and phrases are used are for effect.
- Note how headings are used to summarise the content on each page.
- Complex sentences such as: *'Landslides can occur and fires can start if power cables and gas lines are broken.'* (page 15) employ subordinate clauses to convey more than one idea.

Word meaning and spelling

- Distinguish between the different styles used in the main text and the 'voice' of the scientific expert (for example, in providing additional information).
- Unfamiliar, technical words (such as *'tsunami'* and *'tremors'*) are explained in the text and in the glossary.

Curriculum links

Geography – Look at websites and other non-fiction sources to explore regions mentioned in the text (such as San Francisco in America) and look at measures taken to prepare for earthquakes.

PSHE – For regions where an earthquake may have occurred recently, children could find ways to support the relief effort such as holding a school sale or through collecting clothing and bedding to send. Children can write posters to advertise events.

Learning Outcomes

Children can:

- read silently most of the time
- explain and evaluate use of the organizational features used to convey information
- draw together information from across the text to summarise what has been read
- express reasoned opinions about what is read, relating to own or others' experience.

A guided reading lesson

Book introduction

Give a copy of the book to each child. Read the title and the blurb together and then ask each child to silently read pages 2 to 5 to themselves.

Orientation

Ask the children to summarise what they have read on these first pages, demonstrating when necessary: *These first two pages tell us what it feels like to be in an earthquake. What words are used to describe it? Do you think these words are effective?*

Establish that this text is a non-fiction report. Review the features children would be expecting to see: *Now have a flick through – what features can you find?* Children may notice the absence of a table or chart.

Preparation

Contents page: In pairs, ask the children to predict what each section will be about. For example, *what will be included in a section headed 'Be prepared'?* Take the children into the text to confirm their predictions.

Page 6: Look at the diagram and read how the author uses a simile of an egg to describe this. Evaluate how effective this is to describe what happens. Could the children describe it another way?